new ballads
rod mckuen

rod mckuen

·

new ballads

STANYAN BOOKS

RANDOM HOUSE

BOOKS BY ROD McKUEN

NEW BALLADS

Stanyan Street and Other Sorrows

For the most part, these songs were written during the last week of December and the first week of January of this past year. They are meant to be song lyrics and were written to music — therefore, they are only poetry when they are being sung.

R.M./May 1970

as i love my own

Your smile as it widens on your face
is like a child running off across the hill.
And I love your smile
as I love my own.

Your hair climbing down around your ears
has never been more beautiful than now
and I love your hair
as I love my own.

Your body moving down to mine
is like the coupling
of the pale November clouds
and I love your body
as I love my own.

And I love your body
and it's part of my own.

all i need

How many people
have so much to live for
how many people, indeed
can say to the daylight
that eats up the darkness
I've got all I need.

Mornings and evenings
clear through the night-time
I go wherever you lead
yours is the face
yours are the shoulders
and your hand's all I need.

Turning my clock to the wall
I fall down in your arms.
Then like the phoenix
I rise again
your touch my only alarm.

So once in the morning
and once in the evening
I look in your eyes and I read
enough love to last me
the rest of my lifetime
all I'll ever need.

thank you for christmas

Thank you for Christmas
the first one I remember
that was more than just another day
deep in December.
Back came the holidays
the ones I told goodbye
until you paused a moment
and looked me in the eye.

And thank you for what I thought
I'd never find
Christmas of a kind
I'd conjured in my mind.

As for the lights of town
like Christmas down the hill
off beyond your nakedness
I can see them still.
I supposed that I knew even then
Christmas is for little boys
and not for grown-up men.

Still for a time in the year
that we've just passed
I wanted you to know
you gave me Christmas at last.

and tonight

1.
Because the sky is black
as black as most goodbyes
I've come to see what light
I might find in your eyes
tonight.

Because the world is empty
and because I'm empty too
I've come to be here
for a while and look at you
tonight.

Because my new life now
is lived inside your smile
I've come to talk to you
and stay awhile
tonight.

I have no compass and no chart
no way of knowing where to end
or where to start
I must rely on you
if I can't depend on my own heart.
And so, I've come here once again
to talk to you
tonight.

And tonight
everything is all right.

2.
Because tomorrow's arms
are already real
I've come to find out
how a friendly touch can feel
tonight.

Because your back
can hold off even dawn
I thought I'd use it
as the boat that I sailed on
tonight.

Here with your head
against my chest
whatever else there is
I'll forget the rest
tonight.

I know no reason and no rhyme
no need of keeping track
of tide or time,
since I discovered you.
God knows what else I'll find
here close to you
tonight.

And tonight
everything is all right.

3.
Because you smell like yesterday
I thought I'd come here
once again and stay
the night.

Because my arms have ached too long
I thought I'd rest them here
where they belong
tonight.

Because if I'm anything at all
I'm part of you
however small
tonight.

I have no compass and no chart
no way of knowing where to end
or where to start
I must rely on you
if I can't depend on my own heart
and so, I've come here once again
to love you
tonight.

And tonight
everything is all right.
And tonight
everything is all right.

and i looked at you a long time

And I looked at you a long time
before I left
thinking how beautiful you sleep.
And so I wouldn't waken you
I dressed in the darkness
and covered you against the morning cold.

And I looked at you a long time
before I left
and once more before I turned to go
I turned back again
to be sure I could remember
you doubled up in drunken darkness.

And I wrote a note and left it in on
    your mirror
I said *I'll think of you this morning
when I shave.*
And going down the driveway
grumpy with love
I stole your Sunday paper.

And I looked at you a long time
before I left
and I paused on each and every stair
knowing I might never climb that
   stairway again
I looked at you a long time.
Now everytime I shave
I find myself seeing you again.

i'm not afraid

1.
One afternoon, I came to hear
You sing a soft song into my ear.
Who would have thought, quite by chance
We might engage in the loving dance
Coming together, coming apart
Lost in diversions, dancing starts,
Caught in the quiet, off on our own
Coming together, staying alone.

Are you afraid?

I'm not afraid.

2.
What about you, what about me?
Two years from now, where will we be?
Each of us gone our separate ways
Lost in the headlong passage of days
Maybe we might give love a try
Extending the minutes before goodbye
And for a gentle moment in time
We'll take what pleasure people can find.

Are you afraid?

I'm not afraid.

3.
What is for real, what is false?
All of us seem to be caught in a waltz
Turning around, turning again
When will the dancing ever end?
As for us, you and me
Our eyes are open, we can see
Both of us know where we've been
Why must we both go dancing again

I'm not afraid.

Are you afraid?

4.

Come join the dancing,
   come join the waltz
Don't look too closely at my faults
Why can't I die here in your arms
Safe from the night and safe
   from the dawn
Back to the nothing that has no name!
Back to the nowhere from where I came
Don't worry of me, I know where I am
Where I'm going and where I've been
and I'm not afraid.

rock gently

Rock gently, go slow
take it easy, don't you know
I ain't never been loved this way before
So rock me gently
then we'll rock some more.

Some evening, you'll see
we'll rock on endlessly
But for now just rock me nice and slow
Just, rock me gently
till it's time to go.

Mm-mm, ain't that pretty
mm-mm, ain't that nice
for the first time I feel
I'm skatin' on thick ice.

Rock gently, go slow
take it easy, don't you know
I ain't never been loved this way before
So rock me gently
then we'll rock some more.

gone with the cowboys

One day, with any luck
I'll be off again
gone with the cowboys
on the high roads and then
bulldoggin' sunshine
the way I should have been
all these years that I mistook
for livin' settin' in.

I only hope
too much time ain't gone by.
I may not make Montana
but I'll give it a hell of a try.

Soon as the snow clears
I'll be off again
gone with the cowboys
playin' poker with wind
not thinkin' no more
'bout how it might have been
I'll be in there livin'
with the cowboys again.

Sure as the sun sets
and the world
rides on the wind

I'll be ridin' somewhere
with the cowboys again.

Gone with the cowboys again.

philadelphia

1.
Everytime I walk down Sunset
early in the morning
I get to thinkin'
when I walked the whole night through
and it's then I turn my eyes
towards the heavens and thank God
for that morning I awakened
on a pillow next to you.

But I had to leave for Philadelphia.
Why that was I'll never know.
I do believe Philadelphia
is as far away from heaven
as any man can go.

2.
I remember when I left you
early in the morning
I kept on thinkin'
you might have loved me too —
and I drove a little faster
than I did before I knew you
I had learned
that Sunday mornings were all too few.

But I had to leave for Philadelphia.
Why that was I'll never know.
I do believe Philadelphia
is as far away from heaven
as any man can go.

3.
Now, I never fail to see you
each and every morning
I close my eyes
and I can almost feel you there.
What the hell so many men
have never even walked down Sunset.

I was in your arms awhile
so I've been everywhere.

But I had to leave for Philadelphia.
Why that was I'll never know.
I do believe Philadelphia
is as far away from heaven
as any man can go.

tomorrow and today

Chewing on your thumbs
when trouble comes
never helps to eat it away.
You've got to share
the bad times with someone
tomorrow and today.

Looking out to sea
shouldn't just be
another debt to loneliness you pay:
You ought to try
to open up with someone
tomorrow and today.

What troubles you, troubles me.
Didn't you know that
silence can be loud
even in a crowd.
Loud enough to drive love away.
You ought to come out
and play with someone
tomorrow and today.

I only mention that as someone
who intends to be here to stay
tomorrow and today
tomorrow and today
tomorrow and tomorrow and today.

in someone's shadow

There is substance of a kind
in someone's shadow
the inside of the outside of a dream
and when you lie down in the darkness
in the shadow of a lover,
who cares if things are not
what they may seem.

There is safety that is sure
in someone's shadow
you belong to part of something
   you can feel
in the silence of the nighttime
in the shadow of a lover
what matters if reality's unreal.

If we must go as tattered gypsies
seeking out the friendly people
let it be so.

For more than one man has come up
from someone's shadow
and looking back
    before he closed the door
he's found sunlight
    streaming through the window
sometimes when he's lucky he finds more.

hit 'em in the head with love

1.
Some towns have so many islands
you need a boat to go from block to block
and since the sand
   keeps on getting deeper
I'm building my home upon a rock.

And the next time somebody comes along
and knocks me down
I'm gonna get up
and hit 'em in the head with love.

2.

I know some people who ain't much
    for action
they'd rather sit around and merely talk.
But talk is cheap,
and the days are gettin' shorter
so I'm buildin' my home upon a rock.

And the next time somebody comes along
and knocks me down
I'm gonna get up
and hit 'em in the head with love.

3.
I got a bed full of feathers
a hole or two in nearly every sock.
But I don't owe nobody nothin'
so I'm building my home upon a rock.

And the next time somebody comes along
and knocks me down
I'm gonna get up
and hit 'em in the head with love.

4.
I'm crazy for crossword puzzles
so I got my dictionary out of hock
since the nights are gettin' longer
   and longer
I'm buildin' my home upon a rock.

And the next time somebody comes along
to knock me down
I'm gonna get up
and hit 'em in the head with love.

a while more with you

Let me stay a while more with you
There's so much I have yet to learn
Do you like the colors green and blue
Let me stay a while more with you.

Let me walk a mile more with you
There's so many backroads left to see
We can watch them open up anew
Let me walk a mile more with you.

So much of yourself you let no one see
when you're beside me
I wonder how much of me is really me.

Let me share a smile more with you
There's so many smiles I've yet to give
Before you came,
    my smiles were very few
so let me share a smile more with you.

index

ROD McKUEN was born in Oakland, California, in 1933, and grew up in California, Nevada, Washington and Oregon. He has traveled extensively both as a concert artist and as a writer. In the past three years his books of poetry have sold in excess of three million copies in hardcover, making him not only the best-selling poet of this age but probably every other era as well. In addition, he is the composer of more than a thousand popular songs, several film scores, including *The Prime of Miss Jean Brodie* (for which his song received an Academy Award nomination). Artists such as Frank Sinatra, Petula Clark, Glenn Yarbrough, Rock Hudson, Claudette Colbert and Don Costa have devoted entire albums to his composition.

His major classical works, *Symphony #1, Concerto for 4 Harpsichords and Orchestra* and *Concerto for Guitar and Orchestra,* have been performed by leading American symphony orchestras as well as those in foreign capitals of the world.

Before becoming a best-selling author and composer, Mr. McKuen worked as a laborer, radio disc jockey, newspaper columnist and as a psychological-warfare script writer during the Korean War.

He is currently writing screenplays based on his first two books of poetry and is about to make his debut as a film director.

When not traveling, he lives at home in California in a rambling Spanish house with a menagerie of sheep dogs, cats and a turtle named Wade.